Animul/
Flame

Animul/ Flame

Michelle
LEWIS

CONDUIT BOOKS
& EPHEMERA

If you are a woman, writing about your experience of being a woman, you are part of one of the most avante-garde literary movements there has ever been.

Everything that happens in this poem is entirely your fault.

—A.K. Blakemore

ISBN: 978-1-7336020-0-6

Published by Conduit Books & Ephemera
788 Osceola Avenue, Saint Paul, Minnesota 55105

www.conduit.org

Cover photos courtesy the Library of Congress

CONTENTS

Animul Sonnut

I'm three months drinking in the
heat and something in me dead.
Nothing left to sieve me. You beat

me to it. You are running to me,
piece of the shirt you shed tucked
into your waistband. Cocks that crow

when it's still dark lose their heads,
but no one will calm me to this night:
eyes the gun-scope cauldrons we cry

out of, shirt a streamer that my fear
reared snake-like up to lip at.

So I ate my toward and took a throat to it.

They tell me now that this will never choke you.

Animul

What, if anything, to make of the false "u"? The "a" was taken
by true brutes, wolves who went too far, dwelled a pace or two beyond

the timberline. As if that's where danger lived. Those woods were my
redoubt (they held more in than they did out) where boys sang *stop me*

if I go too far, too far itself just another town beyond the quarry.
Animul says if you're grouse turned by the season into game then, well—

it's you yourself who calls you kill. But what is the delight of fruit
if not to bare itself to beasts? Call that wulf right on this account:

little huffing's needed to unbolt an open door. Some house, though—
clubmoss on a russet crust. Time alone would pull it to its floor.

Time Alone

Such a girl. Don't know *cadenza*, don't know *quich*e.
Know *jacklight* and *ICU*. Know in a silo two people
must turn toward one another. The frightened

love the moat time digs. Just standing still won't
make a house. More a grave, dead waiting for the dead.
Time alone would pull it down. Soon: Animul's fist

through the car window, pieces pooling in your
clothes. Rain them into the toilet. Now what.
Now nothing. Stand still and time will reach you.

Cemetery Hill

Pond idle in its earthhole.
Janie gone to babysit for Pervert
Bert. My father at Maine Med,

my mother somewhere
between us. I raised up my knees,
let the pedals spin until I wrecked.

At the bottom, my blood jarred
then roused me. I spit on it: it rubied—
a ruin I could turn in or out.

East Kennebec

Before the Boston brace they said would unbend me.
Before Char hauled the buckets from the wellhouse,
before the blood was coughed up.

Saved for faux silk sheets from Sears.
Allowed to pick tchotchkes from the truck
before they were set for selling.

Doc's journals piled in the carriage house:
a hall of cysts and lesions. Taped up the anorexics
to make a bony coffer inside the closet wall.

Stood inside the walk-in freezer practicing the dark.
Each panic less, each session longer than the last.

Jacklight

At school the Baptist girls asked
of my father *Was he saved?* Our
jacklit deer hanging in their barns.

I cleaved toward the Catholics,
swigged their communal bottles,
mornings pooling overhead.

Handheld lamps, made to catch
the eyeshine. The dead not even
knowing how they died.

Janie

Night hauled the moon
around. We hurled inkwells
at the carriage house chimney.

When I asked *What happened*
when he drove you home
she wrote F-U-C-K with a finger
between girders of the silo wall.

Next: a padlock on the carriage house door.
Summer's tongue at the culvert.

Janie quiet on the bus, the vacant seats rattling,
everything unhinged.

I backed into the dark until fear left me.

Flame

Born in friction and focused light
and what of it? In rums and
cokes in party city.
You know me by
burst into, keeper of the

and both are true.
Blue skin, pine-sap hair
thirsty for oxygen.

I am Flame: my mother
burnt coal, father
a paroxysm, a glistening rivulet
snuffed out.

Taught to survive
and nothing else.

Char's Lesson

Now trees have shaken in the wind where there is
no wind and you must clutch yourself.

You must toggle on your heelbone and become it.

This is how they plot the living: to rove and arc us,
take away our bough, our eros, whatever shell we breasted. To rise
the bottom up and drop it out of me.

Heart merely ash, and the Flame I'm mother to—
it clings, it takes my knees down. I cannot put more blood to it.

Cut, Never Eaten

Crushed cigarettes rotting in the rafters.
That is the picture I love most. In girls
there is blood coming and going.

Inside them, broth seeks its border, an
inkblot: innards doubled like a sycamore's wing,
little plane spun by the wind. Tell me

how to be cut and never eaten, how
to be riddled, a deck of cards. How to be
club and clover and make the hearts grow fonder.

Char Sonnet

At trouble begins the threshold, begins the throb of ash I keep
trying to put out. But you had a daughter, flame whose scarlet gash
enhanced whatever bleakened. So tarred, you burned on when
you didn't want to. Lousy luck our souls were thin from grieving.
Planets on the sun's same side, dime-thin, boned and hung.
Aluminum edges taking the nights apart, some kind of life. That's
how Char became, turned to hissing ground dust. We wasted
white girls in a podunk, infected with the lovers meant to soothe
us, now even our shadows are ridden. Gardener seeding our palms,
saying this much will make you sick, seeding more, saying this much
will kill you. That's what survival came to mean: to weave a master-
piece of holes from ochre silage. Some kind of life. And what is a
Flame without a chuckhole of ignition to set her. You blackening
and blackening your hands as if we'd never stop unclaiming it.

Char's Sorrow

The thing about my mother is I don't think
you understand *cramhole,*   I don't think you understand *back into.*

The thing is take the scissors to bed.

Is what kind of man puts candy in a dish that isn't candy but just mints.

The kind of man she's with
while I'm home, on a farm. I am eleven
          and all this seems like *brave* but really it is *breaking.*

The thing about my mother is between the flowers of the wallpaper
I have written tiny words
and jiminy   it is a garden of the body.
Of crotch and rub and feel me up. So far apart
          no one could know they even   say.

All this seems like succor, when it is really *suck her.*

The thing about my mother is I don't think
you understand   *alone in this acreage of dark*
          where I listen in on the party line   till they say

          someone's there, someone's breathing
          to each other.

The thing about my mother
is this is one way to girl me.   One way to fear-me-not.

Is some of our stuff in his garage.

Is   this body's orchard
saying   teach me how to die
while I'm still living.

Easy Shooting

Father, didn't we get a good
bloodletting when you died.

A mother and daughter alone in
an empty farm was something to know about.

The news passed between men
at Dewey's Store with their
Slim Jims and change.

From inside, we watched them
jacklight deer on our

edgeless farm, acres
collapsing into the timberline

where soon I'd watch the silage rot
over some local boy's shoulder.

They found the eyeshine, beamed it
toward the gleam, stitched those hooves
to ground for easy shooting.

Flame's Relief

Will tonight be every night?

Outside the kick-out door
saying if the dark
then so can I,   saying let someone return.

Saying this looks like *leave hi*m but is really *suck him.*

The dark is the best of all the ruptures. Here after the movie where they
flew off the cliff it was nothing like drowning, which is
          the best way, the hair's soft waltz, pocketful of whore-y posies.

How could I
          know? (Don't know *Eames* don't know *aioli.*)

O body, you are fresh as a daisy,
a slow rolling moss outside the drop that's bottomed.

And there it is:
flesh is merely flesh and you can empty it. You can roll
me over. Decide what is too little or too much.
Decide the shine of the nut
or the meat it tosses.
                    Score it.
See how the sweetjuice takes the load off.
See the prism giving up its hues.
Fix yourself / take your gulch and plunge your fixit in.

Rivulet Sonnet

What does asunder mean. When they want me to reveal you
I say you are a ruckus in the trees that bends my attention.
Sometimes I hoard your scattering in my eyes, sometimes every
joint heavens. What protects the knight? One says armor, one says
sword. I paid my debtors in sap, mealed with them unmetaled.
Rubbed raw, I was ready to let anyone. Passed around my palms
before undressing. Then my mouth became a passage to an
amber city that took some lack away. How did we live in so
many rooms, the hoariest of histories. Our past shingles itself
until at last it roofs me and here is the truth it shelters. Do you
want to see the heck of it? Do you want to see what my closet
looks like? I plan to live unfenestrated there. Tethered to its
dresses, I will be ready for the earth you've parted. To make
the ground's furrowing my with. To be finally floored by it.

Notes

1. A mixture of orange peel and motor oil.

2. Not so much a disinterest or rejection of dolls as an acute interest in mechanical things.

3. Others were "little hobo," "dear one," and "Merv."

4. After assessing his age and overall health, she feels certain she can outrun him.

5. Also referred to as "the soft papaya of her ear."

6. *A Shred of Dignity*, self-published.

7. Later, the mother called and explained that although she had not read it, she had in fact thumbed through the book, and asserted that there were misrememberances and factual errors. For example, she pointed out the brief story concerning the incident that took place over pancakes, explaining that the restaurant in question never served breakfast, so the tale could not have been true.

8. A cook at the restaurant, 1974–76.

9. This could be the range of a human voice or a musical instrument, or alternatively, any of the varieties of a language that a speaker uses in a particular social context.

10. Ibid, the latter.

11. Not so much a metaphor as an illustrative image, or as a critic has stated in reference to Anne Carson, "the overall action of the mind rather than the high-shine lacquer of the apt image."

12. Blood almost certainly didn't actually "ejaculate out [sic]" of the wound. While there was a dangerous amount of blood loss over time, to be consistent with the injury as well as the altitude, the blood would likely have seeped or possibly oozed.

13. The meaning of the word "stay" is twofold. "Stay" is intended in the sense of staying put, but also in the sense of creating a stay, as "a stay against ordinary childhood loneliness."

14. There may have been days in which they made and ate breakfast there (it is probable that dishes would have included pancakes), though the restaurant did not officially serve it.

15. Perhaps an infant or someone who has had too much cough syrup.

16. An apparent reference to an earlier line that appears in the chapter *Heartburn in a Mexican Restaurant*: "accosted by this gray moment." The color gray makes other appearances by way of multiple references to the "oxidized sky" in the chapter *God Bless the Father* and in reference to the eyes of the father (blind to color, to forgiveness).

17. The Euler Line, or, with denotations as stated, $\sin 2A(B - C)x + \sin 2B \sin (C - A)y + \sin 2C \sin (A - B)z = 0$.

18. While the final section creates a sense of closure, it is by any assessment a conclusion that is a touch facile—that is to say, letter-perfect in its own reckless way.

19. Unreadable, but widely believed to be "licked."

20. Less a "connecting of dots" than a widening and a subsequent flinging of dots around the resulting chasm.

Fabled Storm

How can a storm be fabled?

An ordinary man leaves in rough
weather to bring a goat to shelter.
Every paper pasture, every edge his non-ending.

What will be my radiance
now? Who will I vine my violets to?

O jiminy, what a cross you've hawked,
you've healed, to put the bear on me.

Animul / Flame

Animul owned the sun that beat
the back of the gavel-nosed deer.

Around us, sweetbread mountains with
their anatomical stone stone stone.

I was Flame, a fig wasp hunched in her own
sky. Sunrise tasted of red gums and spittle.

I stood at the bars of night, kneed
the floor, thought that would dismantle it.

Some nights I'll half awake as if still
sleeping in that bloom and wither bed.

Ophelia as Sea Urchin

1.

To say I was aloft upon a branch and fell
to rummage in a garden sewn by kelp
is as good an origin story as any.

Men don't know nuance anyway.
Enough for them to say my anus is
my center and I am full of honey.

They still harvest me from above,
net and pull me, hundreds to a single
hand. Unhumaned, enspined, it's how

they've schooled me, how I know to make
my storyline my own. Such as: The world
is my mantle and I chew through stone.

2.

Is madness always grief?

What if love provoked me, if
the constant ebb and flow were
merely dizzying, as champagne?

Now I populate a world
not kinged by heads, and so
it comes unriddled: When a
man is at odds with a woman
then she is mad. My madness
was desire whetted on the stone
of womanhood, not a spurning.

I thought I was nothing without
that scrim of blame, but now
the truth—it floods my mouth.

3.

The tide unvirgined me (at
last) but I was not its vessel.
All my insides outside.
What passes through my tongue
just glorious milk.

And that's when I changed,
took off that brutal wrenching
I was hostage to when love
was something done to me.

Gameplay

We played When The Lips Are Silent The Fingertips Chatter.

We played Blood Moving From The Extremities In Fight
Or Flight Makes Them Itch
And Then You Rub Them.

I was elated from my novice wins, though they seemed
less a tally than a crack you slip through.

Then, instead of Grooming Gestures
(touch an errant hair and you're out)

and Leniency Or Punishment (a sort of
abstract Jenga with a twist),

we played Did You Drive A New Way Home.

We played There Might Be Some Cameras.
With Animul's thumbs at the pulse of my wrists,

my victories unraveled. The Cluster Rule,
The Dire Hour, Where Does The Blood Go.

Self-Portrait with Antanagoge

Not hungry, but always on the menu.
Not silken, but perfect for a prince:
has some delinquency, some drowning.
Milk but no butter, silt settled in the britches.

What's more, no prince—but serves paper
in a handshake, opens the glove, says there is
no weapon there. If a weapon, then no shield.

No warrior, but gripping with the knees.

Ophelia as Sea Urchin and the Lost Dogs

So this is marriage by a blade:
a tiny frill and bloodless. I am
no different from the sky / the sky.

Still, something spines me—
where are the wild dogs I tamed?
It was a kindness I liked keeping.

Now I'm pronounced, taste of metal.
I respirate, I let my body jewel.
I learn (every day) to let them go.

Drowning

They say it is the best way to die: the hair's soft waltz,
a prism giving up its hues. Pockets overfull with the stones

of old lessons. *Believe me, you wouldn't want to be president*,
my mother used to say. We were always breathing

in our separate rooms. *Just get by*, yet I could feel
myself dying. Tonight, her voice is asleep under the clay.

Across the wall, light unfurls—my neighbor returning
from his lover's house already sipping at that dark that can

empty you. *There are things worse than death* we repeated then,
dead in our own skin, head propping up our fearful faces.

Flame Wants to Make a Call

These are the remains of Animul's career in law enforcement:
Confiscated VHS tape from drug bust.
Camelhair brush for evidence dusting.
Phone taps with tiny suction cups to nurse on private stories.

There is a phone booth on the corner. In it,
the comfort of a thousand fingerprints.

On the tape, women have sex with a series of different animals.

The Amber

What we feel most has no name but amber, archers, cinnamon, horses, and birds.
—Jack Gilbert

If I could make it any clearer I would:
the amber is bat-shit crazy.
We scream at the dogs to stay away
from the amber.

The amber was built for distance. Old folks say
they are "caught up in the amber."

It's always in the spring of its endurance.
It feels only the rock
it's wrapped around.

The amber shot the president in a warehouse
and was caught in a theater. The amber
shot the president in a theater
and was caught in a warehouse.

The amber always takes me to a second location.

I thought the amber was my reckoning, that it
would bury me. But the thing you can't bear
breeds affection for the thing. Now the amber

is keeping me alive. I wish
I could say it better: it's not
as much a torrent as a tether.

Ophelia as Sea Urchin Looks at Photographs

There is the frame, for one thing.
Hemming out the moon.

There's a man dancing, or else his foot
is sliding something sharp out of reach.

Here he's running, has spied something
with his scooped-out eyes. I don't know

the woman—she seems ordinary,
a wingless bird with muddy shoes.

What a shame about the desiccating light.
It's forced a slick of applejack across the faces.
They want me to mistake them: as likely

held in hope as in a ditch. And to be gazed
upon even *after* death? That I couldn't know.

The end does crave a place to bring its thirst,
and underwater is a kind of death I've come
alive to. Still, past those manmade symmetries

they've been cornered by—gardens must spill
their fruit there. O jiminy, they must stun us.

Flame Makes a Call

1.

Do you remember how the needle
drifted in that glossy ungrooved space before it soared
back to the beginning,
I asked J.

I had come down to the phone booth to call.

Do you remember how when we ruined
it was inside that glossy silence?

It could absolutely happen
that I could find out that A had met with J
and was told we could not ever talk again because of something that made
    a kind of sense.
Because that also happened with B.

And it absolutely did happen
J said.

at McDonald's, the sunglasses with the lanyard, how A looked like a
    sleestack in them,
how J was creeped out but not scared as if having walked briefly into
a weird movie before walking back out of it.

I said I think the phone booth could be bugged.
J said do you think you are going mad?

That hush between All For Leyna and You May Be Right again.
Between For Cryin' Out Loud and Two Out of Three Ain't Bad again.
When I go downtown, I said, the merchants' eyes are turning.

2.

Do you remember the big knob we'd unspool across the dial,
the eye to its glass toothy grin as if
there was another world outside of this one and if you could find someone
there you could touch it,

I asked J and wondered aloud how I'll ever learn if I'm not taut.
J said you have to taut yourself.

I said I want to cut myself
out of myself. I said I want to be held down by something.

3.

Remember Doc's old jars, how that rancid fluid always had something
    floating,
how once we found two tonsils in formaldehyde and we left them on the sill
then we looked and looked because we knew somewhere
there had to be an embryo.

J said are you moated?

I said I'm very castled, very fabled.
I want to come back down here with my dime and wring you.

J said why do fingerprints on the phone worry you?
I said because I'm so taut I don't know what is true.

Then J said where'd you go? I said to A, whose tools are truth and logic,
who is both char and glisten. I said
remember those books where the answers to the questions

were printed upside down. I said
he is oxygen to me.

Then J said this is a shitstorm.

4.

Remember crawling on the roof of the barn, waiting for that malt liquor
    sunrise
I asked the truth police,

        who said you don't have to have a spear to stick yourself.
        They were always leaving their card in case I remembered something.

When they said *What's your name*
just like that I was Flame again,

and that's all I can remember except
up the scared-ass stairs like a goat and all the blood draining.

Flame's Lessons

Outside Animul's door
I was part black at the
edges, part *Don't say please.*

What is grouse if not game?
The question hardened to a crust in the night air.

I would be what I was, part char
and cheatgrass, wanting to be set on fire,

wanting not to be a pulse
ticking in a wrist.

Brazenness had fathered me
—a rivulet igniting—
it surged. Father, false start

that left us rocking like grass above the earth,
I am belfried with the swell of you.

The black ash of my hands:
taught to survive and nothing else.

But that's not true.

Learned to jump the tailgate
when the truck slowed.

Learned to stash Merits
in the eaves.

Learned to know a fire when I saw one.

Notes

21. Symptoms included mouth speaking like a child, "like a deafness," and bouts of intense paranoia concerning the phone, taps, and the monitoring, cohorts "watching" or "filming" or performing dubious and unnecessary "terry stops" or "traffic stops" on the part of police or "colleagues."

22. There is precedent for this in populist self-help literature: when a person finds their "other," they are like "twin flames" which, when joined, make a single flame.

23. Between the bourbon and the daybed.

24. The remaining unquoted is attributed to Joseph Heller and is, "[...] doesn't mean they aren't after you."

25. It is common to think that the jacklit deer wants to flee but cannot because of some sort of physical effect it is unable to overcome, or that it is immobilized with fright. This is not true. In fact, upon being lit, its vision is flooded so it is unable to see human movement and, as such, it does not feel threatened. The deer stares at the light unmoving, seemingly hypnotized (though not, in fact, immobilized) and can be easily shot.

26. The inference is that if they did/could flee, they would not know toward what or in what direction.

27. Hence, a rivulet makes earth into a kind of grave with its parting. Also, Rivulet, father to Flame.

28. The eyeshine of different animals are different colors. Some common colors are green (dog), yellow (deer), and amber (skunk).

29. This is an error, as humans do not have eyeshine because human eyes have evolved to see in the daytime, whereas most animals have eyes that have evolved to see at night.

30. Lamplight hunting is almost always illegal. Hunting is illegal after sunset, exceptions being coyotes in overpopulated regions, alligators (permit needed), raccoons, opossum. *N.B*, hunting is also illegal on "posted" or private land and is illegal within 500 feet of a residence.

31. Also, the illegality of trespass, e.g. driving into one's driveway.

32. Redacted.

33. Inferred.

34. An action performed in order to see the man's name on the registration.

35. *Thelma and Louise.* Dir. Ridley Scott. Perfs. Susan Sarandon, Geena Davis. MGM, 1991. The film was praised for its "uncompromising validation of women's experiences." This was, however, well after its initial release.

36. Likely, the mill roof at Dicker's. They would look for it at the tree line when they were lost.

37. So called.

38. A debt collector or a certified school nurse.

39. This is an approximate location. The silo was nonfunctional, vestibular, fusty. It could be entered on the west side and was used as a sort of hideaway or refuge where privacy was all but guaranteed. Suggests (i.a.) a phallic fixation.

40. Needs citation.

Neither Amber nor Rust

How these birches think they can finger the sky.
I promise, I won't be pretty.
He flushed before we walked out of the bathroom stall
after he cratered our seedhole and licked the sense out of us.
Every man wants his nuts and fruits in silver.
Rubiginous this new ridge, neither amber nor rust.
You want me to be cunt and never eaten?
You want to thin into every oxide hour? Cave yourself.
Unrib the ruptured ticket in your pocket.

The Funniest Thing You Ever Heard

Ha Ha 1: Animul

When Animul asked me to take our flames
& make them into one
I swear to you I thought it was a joke.

I said sure. (I didn't laugh. I was sweeping up a floor.)

This is Animul: stone-eyed,
teeth way in his head (like most
men), tall. Though unlike most (I know
(& I know a lot (another story)))
when angry did
tremble hard his animul head
to show a hell could be un-
leashed but would not be.

Then came the churching: I walked the joke
down a little aisle cottoned in a skirt
with frayed waist edge.

Ha Ha 2: My Afraid

That was the beginning of my afraid.
The end of my a-frayed-and-fairied edges.

Ha Ha 3: The Joke

What makes a joke funny:
not filling the void with laughter.

You have to take the beat
& then it's not the joke:
it is the void that's funny.

Ha Ha 4: Churching

Animul swung me around into the joke, the void.

Some stranger mothering me
from the back

who heard from
a coke-nosed ex about the churching.
That was another edge I made

so funny I forgot to
do a shot of bourbon.
So then I did, left the
    drywall   & the pulloutbed
wore my Easter dress to a job interview.
(Someone shot out a laugh.)

Ha Ha 5: The Joke

It was a joke that broke the window,
a joke that dried the wall.
Maybe bourbon would make this funnier.

Refrain

Don't talk like that / who is that
looking at you / is he from your yoga class? /
your old school? / only use your full and given
name / why is the desk drawer locked? / what
does this piece of paper say? / what do you have
to be a-frayed about?

Ha Ha 6: Rules

Thin & thinner lines broken
& then stretched until
some smithereens: glass in my clothes from
the window that doesn't stretch but breaks.
Pieces in my underwear, what's
the story says the man at the garage. It's sort of funny.
If everything's so much
a rule everything's so many broken. Until:
a day, another severing.

Ha Ha 7: The Funny

Animul said I could call whomever
but they wouldn't take it seriously (was a deputy, knew everyone!
   served papers folded
in a handshake!) Ha ha!
Now you tell me that's not funny.

Ha Ha 8: Inside

Tell that one again:
I'm walking back from _____'s
house without much
of the bourbon left in me,
Two cites (titties) away (astray).

A girl has got to hitchhike
or else how's a girl to get home that far?
Someone seems nice & takes me
to where I pull the bed out of the (dry) wall.
I check his registration from the glove
when he goes in to pay for gas

(just in case—I'm far inside it now,
half bourbon, half bad ass, half something severed).

Against a rule I fray. I bourbon someone's breath.

Ha Ha 9: Done In

Make whoopee pies
watch TV a bit, push the pulloutbed
back in, sleep in the space it left
everything as it had been / or else done in.

Chorus

I heard the joke at the gym
some months hence: Animul had tried
to church the other instructor first
who was prettier, but found out
she was not as lost so I was
chosen.   Ha ha,
you have to laugh because it's
funny. Funny as hell, so funny
I throw up in the bushes behind
the 7-11 where I stop to buy
a Sprite & a balloon. Funny cause
they look at me then through.
Funny cause it's true.

Ha Ha 10: Chosen

Made a cardboard cutout of a sparrow, hung it on the drywall.
Wore my Easter dress to work.
Baked the truth into some poems for Animul's psychologist.

Do tell, said the psychologist
& smiled like a joke had cracked between us.

No snow & so only the sun is
ruin. So lost. So flame. So chosen.

Ha Ha 11: Outside

Animul locked me out because of
the hitchhiking, because what name
on the registration because the sparrow
hanging overhead. Because the movie.

It was about two women
who did not respect their flames
then drove off a cliff.
I was cold, I paid, went in. Was them that done me in.
Animul figured I took a lesson.
Thought I was out thinking.
Cracked a hole in the drywall
where my head
had been. I mooned outside all night.

Ha Ha 12: The Punch(line)

I wasn't even watching (the guns! Brad Pitt!).
I was (from above) watching only me: each direction peopled with
our flames: our ticketed hours: my own church to
clutch the dun in / dark in

Now not even the void is funny.

Here Is the Sea to Drive You Home

Someone knocked and said it's time.
Someone said will you drive yourself home.
Someone said there was no way to

know the sex, a thing that had not
occurred to me to know. Sometimes
we say brave when we mean blood.

A certain pulse still daughters my sky.
How do I ruby the ruin of it. The past
gets hungrier with age—I've turned

my tongue in, broken off my arms
for its eating. I'm no different: bravery
tossed its babies from the boats

when they were drowning. I know
they were thinking *maybe*—a chance
they'd wreathe the shores like stones,

that sun could still ignite them. And
here is the hand you thought you'd lost,
and here is the sea to drive you home.

What Shall We Call Her?

Let's call her half alive,
call her skin a dark
slick of damask. Her eyes,

two lunettes lifting from
her frog head. Half
inside a snake's mouth

one leg protrudes, then
nothing happens, a stone
silence sticks itself to air.

Could have been yesterday
you drifted, a sylph, through
the flea market, a bank

of jeweled crosses wanted
you. You bought an old
-fashioned book with

patty-cake, we thought
there was a baby. Let's
never say *baker* or *butch*er

only *stick* and *candle*.
Let's let float the rest
—an abandoned ship—

out to sea. Let's let her go:
those tiny inkwells no longer
eyes, that pond just the

shithole where she swam.
Below that, *light wrestling*
there incessantly with light.

Migration

This is how to count but
            not to measure:
a small gland in the skull seeps, spills a voyage
in us. Wants to take us to the next reticulum of land.

This is how to know a concrete box
            and still want to wing free.
            Lap, lap,
then lift your head: that same plastic island
       and a tree. Lap, lap,
and lift your skirt—beneath it is
the throat.
The more you go the less I
       no, no silver
sea but in a kitchen kettle.

So why this engine in
the ribs? Why this voice beyond
what we can vessel?

Instructions

You buried something beneath this tree—a jar of muck
that says *Wash your hands in me.* As if you knew who you
would be again.

Note the pelts upon this path. The wind will strew them.

Find the podunk where you cross, field to field,
beyond the wormers who trespass to the flats, know them
from the cups they've lined up on the fender.

Should disorder take the reins of violence,
take off headlong for the crossing. No one goes there.

Waking Life

It's said dreams are the theater where we
play every role

—that's your hand up your blouse, that's
you jimmying doors

at the same pace you're latching them.
I'm not here to say how

to exit your life. There's that Paul Simon song.
That tale of Cerberus, hellhound

of honey cakes. You've got the drug
box, the confections.

You've got the Angie Dickinson pantsuit,
the *I'm Audi 5000 boys*,

I'm histoire, got the radio on Splitsville all
the way to Palooka.

Or don't leave at all. Get tossed out when
that boy you know lingers

and takes you too long, cry like a nighthawk
under that outhouse hole

of a sky. First you're the boy, then you're
the fire erupting,
then you're the pinbones of cold that
ferry the air, then you're the air.

Char / Flame

Night has swallowed enough:
when you set the rum & coke into its
sweaty circle I was clocking,
took my arm and led me to the car,

the streets may have been ash,
snow or dander. Again, the pillar
you backed into. Again, the jolt that
only strengthened your resolve.

Let's say it was our most heroic act.
That we are no different from the brave.
We have our grief and our blood. Let's
say it was our last glass, our last run.

Sonnet for Flame's Apartment

> *Baffling combustions are everywhere!*
> —Ted Berrigan

Third floor. Navy pilot in 302 lets his
metal door crash into its jamb. Pipes wake
inside the drywall to guzzle his water, which I let

mantle me. Below, bank workers jostle toward
cars minutes from their make-believe beds.
Water warming in its iron belly, clock radio

popping through the walls: time wastes us then
takes its beat, curls the linoleum then fills its edges
with the slough of skin and kitchen flour.   What gracious holding!

Come July, a band, and upstairs always the door's
crash! then everything jangling on the shelves as if
nothing can quiet, as if it wants to give itself away.

In Truth

In truth, I pleaded still. I did not make it clean.
I signed the papers *Go to Hell*, wrote *I do not have*
anything worth anything on the Assets line.

Tonged the stainless bins of the salad bar. Watched a Sunday morning show,
then wrote a letter saying *Shame on you* about their condescending
   interview with The Rock.

Blinked against the flash of *Last call for alcohol,*
           then up the stairs, past the graffiti'd mail slots

to drink from my hands over a bathroom sink wreathed with the suite of
   soapstone boxes
I'd had to store because he said people only used them for storing pot.
   Stored pot.

Accepted a beer from between the balusters of the deck
then went inside and poured it down the sink, unsure whether thirst passes
   through you like
                         a breath or runs past you
                         like a train.
Snaked the cable down the hall to the bedroom.
Slept in the room with the window when the sultry air
fixed itself inside the mortar of the walls.   Met a man
who worked the first shift at the Yard,
the pale tract of his skin against the sheets we slept in so beautiful
                      it made me terrified of beauty.

               And what is agency? What you give yourself?
Summer's tongue at the culvert. A ruin to be turned in or out.

I changed the *H-e-l-l* to my name and licked it closed.

Flame's Dream

It is 1990 in a deployed town.
I wear the dress to the interview, its
broad white bib like a side-table linen.

When I exit the building, Animul
runs to me as if I am engulfed in flame.
And so I must be.

In the dream: I'm on the farm,
my mother at the bottom of the stairs,
youthful and not yet char.

She is wet, as though having fallen
into a pond or well and I awaken.

Animul comes home
with tail on fire, is insatiable for knowing.

Rivulet / Flame

When I die it is the night I die to:
chased by a police car for speeding

you banked onto a dirt road,
killed the lights, told me, *Duck*.

In the dark one must learn
where to lay their unfixed eyes.

I held two stuffed animals.
We crouched into the seat.

Take the words you saved and put them here.

The siren seeped its stain
into the sky, an empire

unfolded in my ribs. Exhilarating
now, the blood I was born to.

We were always traveling at night.

ACKNOWLEDGEMENTS

Bennington Review: "Animul Sonnut" and "Time Alone"

Jet Fuel Review: "Animul," "Jacklight" and "Janie"

DASH Literary Journal: "Cemetery Hill"

So to Speak: "Animul/Flame," "Flame's Lessons," and "Instructions"

Your Impossible Voice: "Char's Lesson," "Flame's Relief" and "Char's Sorrow"

Conduit: "Easy Shooting"

Poor Claudia: "Char Sonnet," "Flame Makes a Call" and "The Amber"

Drunken Boat: "Rivulet Sonnet"

Horse Less Review: "Notes (A mixture)" and "Notes (Symptoms)"

Blunderbuss: "Gameplay"

Indiana Review: "Ophelia as Sea Urchin"

Denver Quarterly: "Self-Portrait with Antanagoge"

Up the Staircase Quarterly: "Drowning"

Spoon River Review: "Ophelia as Sea Urchin Looks at Photographs"

LUMINA: "Neither Amber nor Rust" and "Cut Never Eaten"

Feminist Wire: "The Funniest Thing You Ever Heard"

Juked: "Flame's Dream"

Stirring: A Literary Collection: "Waking Life"

WSQ/Feminist Press: "Here is the Sea to Drive You Home" and "Migration"

"Waking Life" appeared in the chapbook *Who Will Be Frenchy?* (dancing girl press, 2016).

NOTES

"Notes (A mixture)" and "Notes (Symptoms)" owe a debt to
David Foster Wallace.

"Gameplay" takes some of its games from *Spy the Lie: Former CIA Officers
Teach You How to Detect Deception* (2013, St. Martin's Griffin) by Philip
Houston, Michael Floyd, and Susan Carnicero.

"The Funniest Thing You Ever Heard" owes a debt to Olena Kalytiak Davis.

"What Shall We Call Her?" ends with a line taken from Hart Crane's
poem, "Voyages."

"Migration" was inspired by an article in *SF Gate* titled "Zoo Penguins Intent
On Futile 'Migration,'" and reads in part: *Brainwashed by six newcomers
from Ohio, 46 penguins at the San Francisco Zoo have abandoned their
burrows and embarked on a great migration—except their pool is not exactly
the coast of South America and there's really nowhere for them to go. [...] Now
they swim most of the day and stagger out only at dusk."*

"Sonnet for Flame's Apartment" includes language taken from Ted Berrigan's
"Sonnet LV," which includes the lines:

> *Baffling combustions are everywhere!   we hunger and taste
> And go to the movies   then run home drenched in flame
> To the grace of the make-believe bed*

My heartfelt gratitude goes to the readers and teachers who are, implausibly,
always there to support me, especially Anita Clearfield, Marcia Brown,
Baron Wormser, Susan Miller, Terrance Hayes, Gray Jacobik, and Laure-
Anne Bosselaar. Thank you for your mentorship and friendship. Thank you
to Bob Hicok. I am extremely grateful to Paula Cisewski, William Waltz,
William Stobb, Scott Bruno, and all the wonderful people at Conduit Books
& Ephemera. You are my true dream team.

Thank you to the caring staff members of the journals who published my work from their slush piles. You do heroic work. Thank you also to the Maine Arts Commission for their valued support.

This book exists because of Arielle Greenberg, who taught me new ways to live and write in this world and about the importance of saying it. I am deeply grateful.

My gratitude to David, my most consequential reader. I love you and our life.

As always, thank you, Richard Aldridge. I wish you were here to see this.

ABOUT THE AUTHOR

Michelle Lewis has worked as a writer, editor, and digital marketer. Her poetry has appeared in many journals, including *Bennington Review, Indiana Review, Spoon River Poetry Review,* and *Denver Quarterly,* and her reviews and essays have appeared in *Gettysburg Review, Electric Lit,* and *Rain Tax*i among others. She is a contributing writer for *Anomaly.* She earned her M.F.A. from the Stonecoast Creative Writing Program. She lives in Maine. You can find out more about her at whitechicken.com.